The Obstacle Course

Written by
Maria Kennedy

Illustrated by
Colleen Crawford

It was my turn for the obstacle course.
I thought the obstacle course was hard.
"You can do it," said my Dad.
"Maybe," I said.
"But I think the rope swing
is too hard for me."

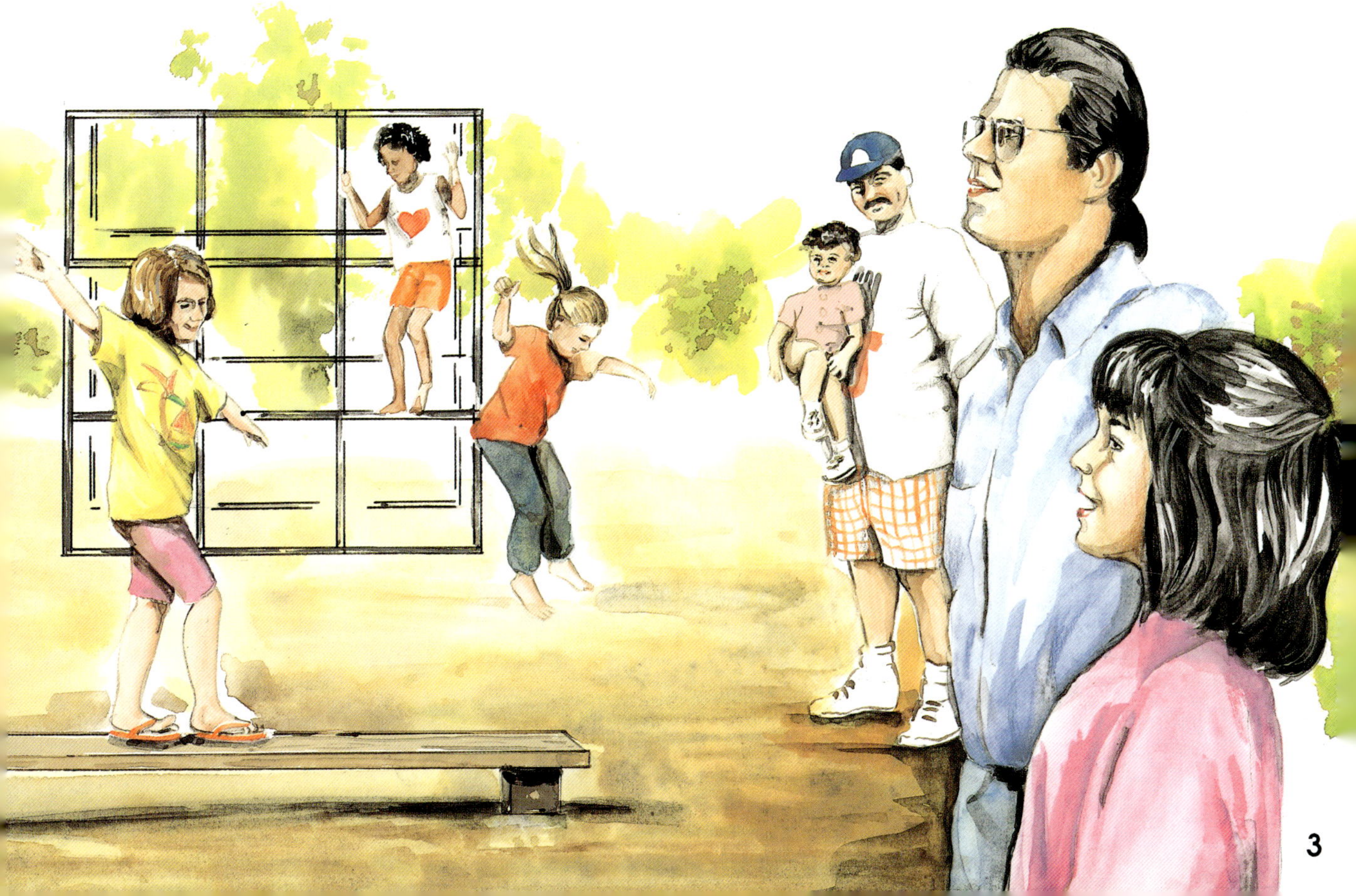

The whistle blew.
I looked at my dad,
and he looked at me.
I hung from the rope swing.
I let my feet leave the ledge.
I flew above the ground.

"You can do it," yelled my dad.
"Aaaah!" I yelled back.
Wow! I COULD do the rope swing.

5

I crawled under the net on my stomach
until I reached the other side.
But there were the climbing ropes.
They were hard,
and they went up high.

7

My dad said, "You can do it."
Maybe I could.
I looked back at my dad.
He was waving to me.
I took one step at a time.
Up, up, up.
I thought I could make it to the top.
Yes, yes, yes.

I went over the top
and landed on the mattress.
I was doing it. I could do it.
I really COULD do it.

I jumped over the tires.
I crawled through the tunnels.
I ran to the finish line.
"I knew you could do it," said my dad.
He gave me a great, big smile.

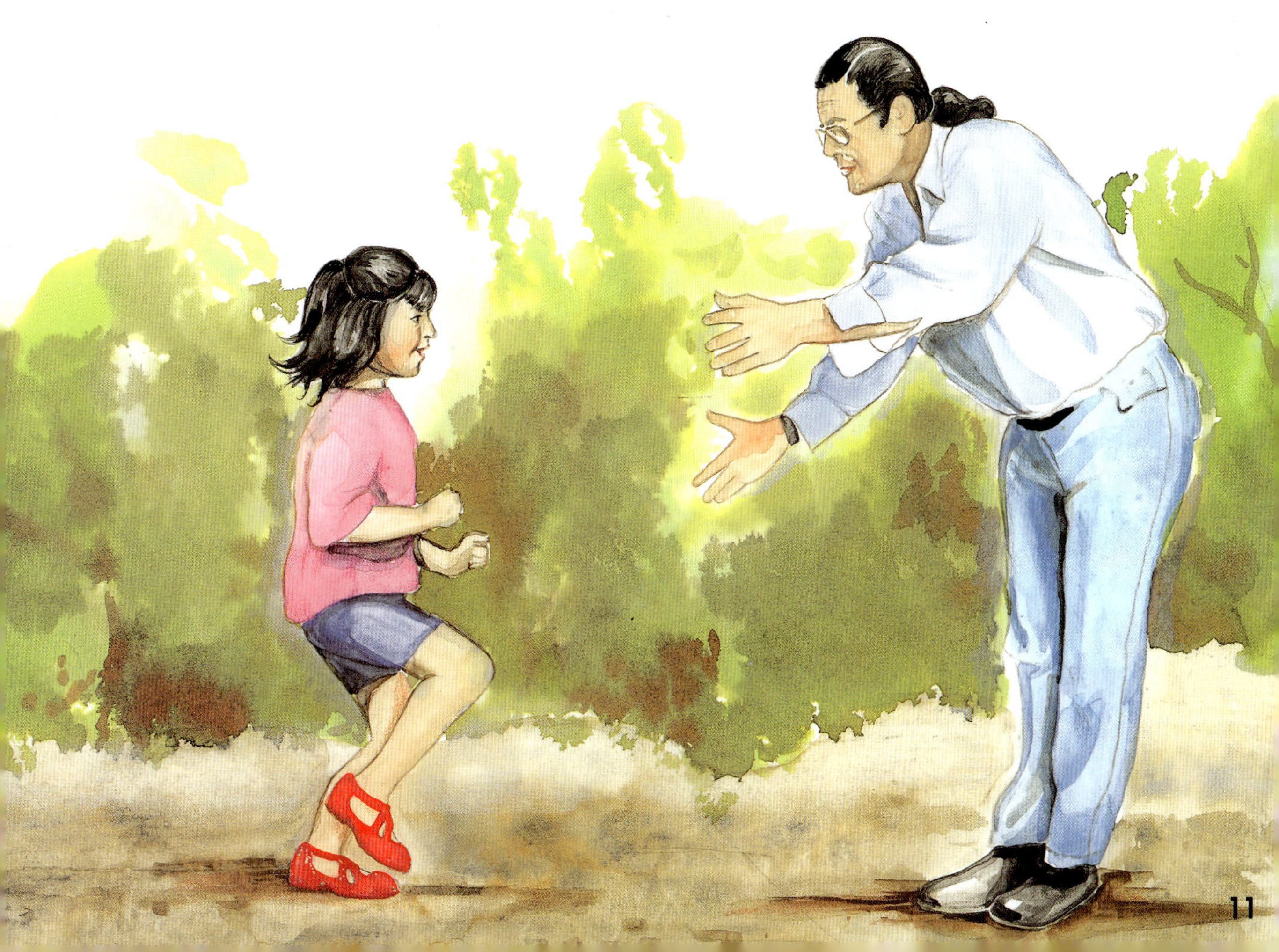

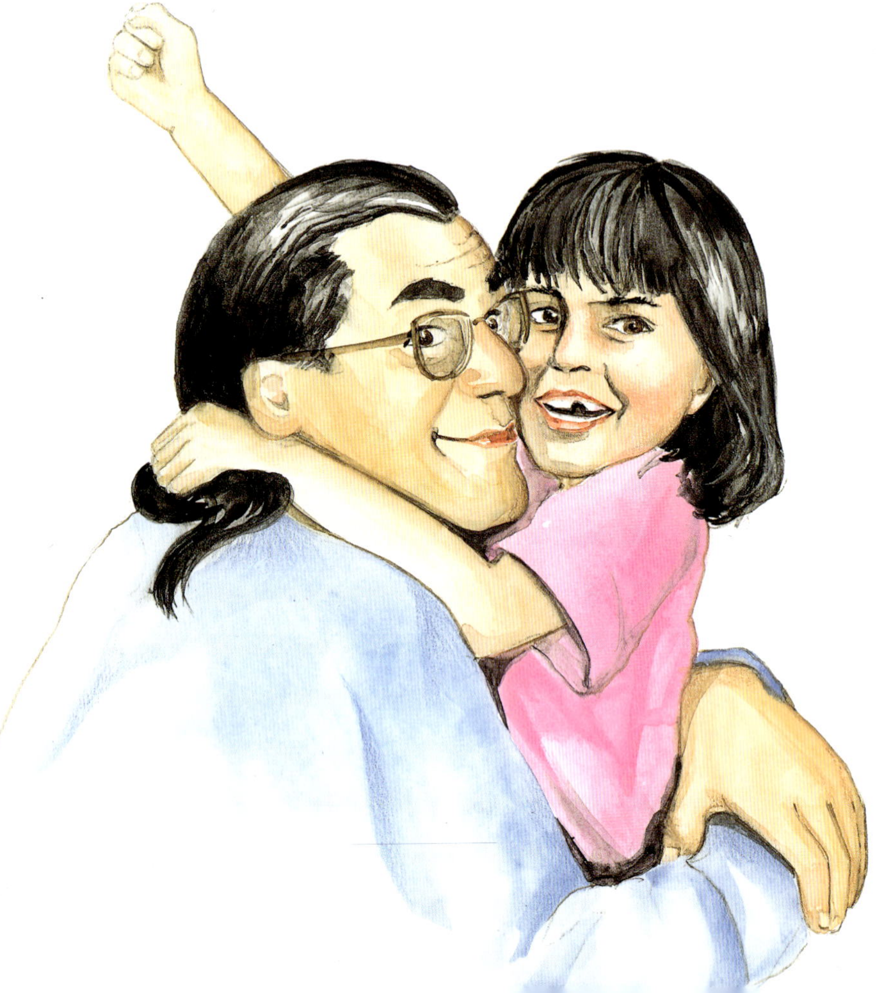